Published by Creative Education
123 South Broad Street, Mankato, Minnesota 56001
Creative Education is an imprint of The Creative Company

Art direction by Rita Marshall
Production design by Clean Tone Creative Consultants

Photographs by: Allsport (Brian Bahr, David Cannon, J.D. Cuban,
Harry How, Hulton Archive, Craig Jones, Ken Levine, Andy Lyons,
Gary Newkirk, Paul Severn, Jamie Squire, Matthew Stockman),
Corbis (Duomo), Getty Images (J.D. Cuban, Scott Halleran, Harry How,
Craig Jones, Ross Kinnaird, Andy Lyons, Newsmakers, Steve Powell,
Andrew Redington, Anton Want), Icon Sports Media (Gary Rothstein,
WireImage.com), Newsmakers (Irwin Daugherty, Joe Raedle),
Timepix (Robert Beck).

Library of Congress Cataloging-in-Publication Data

Goodman, Michael E.
Tiger Woods / by Michael E. Goodman.
p. cm. – (Ovations)
Summary: A biography of the son of African-American and Asian-American
parents who grew up to become a professional golf champion.
ISBN 1-58341-246-8

1. Woods, Tiger–Juvenile literature. 2. Golfers–United States–
Juvenile literature. [1. Woods, Tiger. 2. Golfers. 3. Racially mixed people–
Biography.] I. Title. II. Series.

GV964.W66 G66   2003
796.352'092–dc21
[B]   2002035147

First Edition

2   4   6   8   9   7   5   3   1

OVATIONS

TIGER

WOODS

BY MICHAEL E. GOODMAN

Creative Education

REFLECTIONS

On the evening of April 13, 1997, 21-year-old golfer Eldrick "Tiger" Woods was the guest of honor at the Champion's Dinner following the Masters Tournament. Earlier that day, Tiger had made sports history by becoming the youngest man ever to win the Masters and setting a record for the lowest total score in the tournament's long history. But his accomplishment was even more than an athletic triumph. As the son of parents who were African American and Asian American, Tiger had also made history for people of color throughout the United States. That night, when Tiger stood to receive his applause, it wasn't just his fellow golfers who were clapping. Cooks, waiters, busboys, and dishwashers—many of whom had never watched or played

golf before—also came into the dining hall to join in the cheering. Tiger's victory made them feel proud, too.

Pride and hard work are part of what makes Tiger so special. He has been playing golf ever since he could walk. And he always plays to win. His competitive drive is clear when he puts on a Sunday afternoon charge to come from behind in the last round of a tournament, or when he pumps his fist in an uppercut as he sinks a long putt. Other golfers may feel pressure playing the closing holes. Tiger creates pressure.

Part prodigy. Part warrior. He is a man on a mission to be the best golfer ever and to make golf a sport loved by more people than ever before. "One of my main goals is to make golf look like America," he has said, "played by people of all different races. . . . Why limit it to just a few when it can be enjoyed by all?" For Tiger, there are no limits.

His skill, focus, confidence, and unwavering drive to be the best have earned Tiger a place alongside golf's legends and transformed the sport forever.

EVOLUTION

Earl Woods always knew that his son would be a fearless battler. That's why he began calling the baby "Tiger" soon after his birth on December 30, 1975, in Cypress, California. Earl chose the nickname to honor a colonel in the South Vietnamese army with whom he had served in the Vietnam War. The colonel's name was Nguyen Phong, but everyone knew him as "Tiger." Phong was the bravest man that Earl Woods had ever known.

Tiger's given name was Eldrick, a made-up name that began with "E" for Earl and ended with "K" for Kultida, his mother's name. Kultida, who was brought up as a Buddhist in Thailand, felt that a child whose name showed that he was surrounded by his parents was sure to have good luck.

Tiger received more than luck from his parents. His mother taught

him important Buddhist beliefs about how to live. She encouraged him always to show discipline, respect, and self-control in his actions but also to be a tough competitor, "like a real tiger." His father—a fine college athlete who had experienced prejudice because he was part African American and part Cherokee Indian—taught Tiger to be tough enough mentally to win at sports and to withstand racist comments or treatment.

Earl Woods had another important gift to pass on to his child, a love of golf. When Earl was growing up, only wealthy white people played golf, since golf equipment and golf club memberships were very expensive. Now the game had become one of his passions. "I got hooked on golf the first round I played," he said. "I decided if I had a son, I'd introduce him to golf early on."

In fact, Earl introduced Tiger to golf before he was even a year old. Earl often took his son outside in a highchair while he practiced his golf swing. When the boy began begging for a club of his own, Earl cut down a putter for Tiger to swing. By the age of 18 months, Tiger was able to hit a golf ball hard and straight. At age two, he appeared on a national television show to show off his golf swing. By age three, he was hitting shots expertly out of sand traps. When he was four, Tiger

The strong support of his parents—Kultida, top, and Earl, bottom—has been at the heart of Tiger's career, financially, mentally, and spiritually.

recorded a score of 48 on the back nine holes of the Navy Golf Course, where his father played—better than many adult players.

Tiger was an only child, but he found interesting ways to entertain himself at home and practice golf at the same time. "I turned our living room into a chipping area," he remembered. "I would hit flop shots off the carpet over the coffee table and land the ball short of the fireplace. I never broke anything, though I came close a few times. I had to hit the ball softly, so it made little or no noise, because if Mom heard me hitting balls in her living room, she would have blistered my behind."

Some people began calling Tiger a prodigy—a child with amazing grown-up talents. They compared him to the famous composer Wolfgang Amadeus Mozart. Mozart was composing symphonies by the time he was five years old. Tiger, at the same age, was making his own special music on the golf course.

Unlike most other young golfers, Tiger came from a working-class family, and he played on public courses instead of at country clubs. Tiger's skin was also black, and his heritage was a mixture of African American,

Native American, and Asian. Tiger saw
these differences as making him special.
"My parents have taught me always to
be proud of my ethnic background,"
he once told reporters. "Please rest
assured that is, and always will be, the
case—past, present, and future." Perhaps
it is Tiger's unique background that
has helped make him so popular
among people of all ages and races.

A CHAMPION IN TRAINING

Tiger's golfing ability involved more than natural talent. He also practiced long and hard. Earl invented something that he called "Tiger par" to inspire his son. Tiger wasn't strong enough to complete most holes in the regulation number of strokes for par. So Earl would estimate how many shots it would take Tiger to reach the green and then add two more strokes for putts to determine the "Tiger par" for a hole. Usually the number was six or seven for a normal par-four hole. Tiger worked hard to meet or beat "Tiger par" on each hole.

Another game that father and son played was called "Shotmaker." They would pick an obstacle, such as a tree or rock, and try to hit the ball as close to the obstacle as possible, but not with a straight-on shot. The winner had to hook the ball or vary the angle of the shot, and he had to announce what he planned to do first. Tiger often credits his ability to make some impossible shots today to practice he got in "Shotmaker" games.

Whether in practice or high-profile golf tournaments, Tiger's primary opponent, the person he most wants to beat, has always been himself.

When Tiger was only six, he won his first big tournament, the World 10-and-under Championships. That was just the start. Soon, he was winning events regularly. In 1987, when he was 11, Tiger entered 30 tournaments near his home in southern California and won all 30.

While golf took up most of Tiger's free time, his parents insisted that he keep up with his school work, too. Tiger willingly abided by his parents' rule that he could play golf only after his homework was done—and done right. On weekends, he would spend all day Saturday and Sunday on the golf course and then make sure all his school work was completed by Sunday night.

When Tiger turned 12, Earl Woods decided to retire from his job in public relations so he could accompany his son to tournaments around the country. Kultida continued to work as a secretary, and the couple took out loans and a second mortgage to help pay for golf lessons, equipment, and travel expenses. Tiger's parents felt that his future was worth the cost and sacrifice.

Tiger began building a true national reputation when he turned 15. That was the year that he won the first of three consecutive United States Golf Association (USGA) Junior Championships for players 18 and under. All three times, Tiger had to stage a late-round rally to edge out his final opponent. No opponent's lead was ever big enough to be safe from a Tiger comeback.

Tiger had more than the pressure of winning to contend with during this time. He also experienced a major growth spurt. Over a one-year period, he grew from 5-foot-5 (165 cm) and 110 pounds (50 kg) to 6-foot-1 (185 cm) and 140 pounds (64 kg). The growth meant he had to adjust his swing and the way he kept his body in balance. He also had to switch to longer clubs several times. Still, he made all of the necessary adjustments and kept on winning.

In 1994, Tiger, now 18, entered Stanford University, where he planned to major in business. Tiger, who had an A average in high school, was impressed with Stanford's academic reputation. He also felt that Stanford's golf coach, Wally Goodwin, could help prepare him to win the National Collegiate Athletic Association (NCAA) Championship.

Tiger won his first college golf tournament and within a few months was already ranked as the number

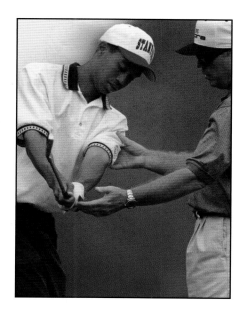

Encouragement from his father, top, and instruction from experts such as coach Butch Harmon, bottom, helped lay the foundation for Tiger's game in the early 1990s.

one college player in the country. Huge crowds began to come out to see Stanford's matches, including many students and minority spectators. That had never happened before. Suddenly, golf was "cool" for people of different ages and colors.

The summer after his freshman year, Tiger scored his biggest golfing victory yet—capturing the U.S. Amateur Championship against some of the best amateur golfers in the world of all ages. Winning the U.S. Amateurs qualified Tiger to play in the Masters for the first time. The Masters, which is held each April in Augusta, Georgia, is one of golf's oldest and most famous tournaments. Very few teenagers or African Americans had ever played in the Masters before Tiger. After Tiger played well in the first two rounds, a group of African-American caddies asked him if he thought a black golfer would ever win the event. Tiger said it would definitely happen someday.

PROFESSIONALLY PREPARED

In 1996, Tiger became the only golfer besides his idol, the legendary Jack Nicklaus, to win both the NCAA Championship and the U.S. Amateurs in the same year. The double triumph convinced him that it was time to turn pro. He began an intensive weightlifting and exercising program to build up

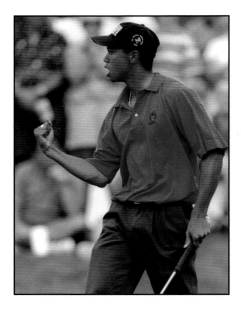

In 1995, Tiger turned heads in the golf world by winning the U.S. Amateurs and qualifying to play in the Masters, an opportunity few African Americans had had.

his strength and stamina. He put on 20 pounds (9 kg) of muscle and was able to hit the ball with more power than ever before. At the same time, he worked on special skill shots he could use to reach the green and get close to the hole, blast out of sand traps, or drive the ball from lies in deep grass, known as "the rough." Tiger now felt he was strong enough and skilled enough to compete against the world's best players.

Tiger officially turned pro at the 1996 Greater Milwaukee Open. He recorded a terrific 67 on the first day of the tournament and even shot a hole-in-one on the last day. He finished in 60th place and earned more than $2,500 in prize money.

In his next three tournaments, Tiger finished 11th, 5th, then 3rd. Before the Las Vegas Open, a headline in *Golf World* magazine asked, "Tiger: How Good Is He?" The next week's headline replied, "He's That Good!" after Tiger roared back in the last round to capture the event on the first playoff hole. Tiger had won his first pro championship. When he won a second event a few weeks later, golfer Peter Jacobson said, "If this is how it is every week, then it's over for the rest of us."

Tiger was already a high-ranked pro golfer, but he was eager to be the best—and that meant winning the Masters. After all, he had made a guarantee that a black golfer could win at Augusta, and he planned to back up his promise.

Nerves got the best of Tiger as he started his first round in the 1997 Masters. He began pushing shots all around the course and finished the first nine holes with a dismal score of 40. No player had ever started out that badly and still won the Masters. But Tiger did just that—in record-breaking fashion. He shot an amazing 30 over the last nine holes to finish day one at 70. He then shot rounds of 66, 65, and 69 for a four-day total of 270. That score was 12 better than the nearest challenger, the largest margin of victory in Masters history. Tiger became the youngest golfer and the first African American to win at Augusta. Just as impressive were the television ratings for the tournament. They set records, too, mostly because millions of young people and African Americans who had never had an interest in golf before had tuned in to watch a remarkable new hero perform.

When Jack Nicklaus was asked about Tiger's Masters triumph, he replied, "Before it's over, he should win at least 10 of these."

Tiger is a power golfer like his idol, the legendary "Golden Bear," Jack Nicklaus, bottom, who holds records for the most U.S. Open wins (4) and most Masters wins (6).

Tiger was on top of the golfing world, but he knew he still had lots of work to do to reach his ultimate goal: "The driving force in my life is to get my game at a level where I'll be able to compete in each tournament I tee up in," Tiger said. Throughout 1998, Tiger and his coach, Butch Harmon, began taking apart and rebuilding his entire game. Tiger worked on every stance and every grip. He wanted to make sure his body was in perfect balance at all times.

Even while he concentrated on improving his golf game, Tiger decided it was time to use some of his money and influence to help minority young people improve their lives. He and his parents established the Tiger Woods Foundation to provide college scholarships for needy minority students, sponsor golf clinics (many of which Tiger personally conducted), and support programs to bring parents and children closer together. The Foundation also joined with Target Stores to co-sponsor a program called "Start Something," which encouraged young people to identify a specific personal desire or goal and begin taking steps toward achieving it. Tiger hoped that some of the youngsters would want to follow in his footsteps on the golf course.

In 1999, Tiger began playing and living with a new style. His tee shots didn't travel as far, but they were more accurate. He had added backspin to his approach shots, so the ball would roll closer to the hole. His putting was even more deadly. He also gave up fast-food for a more healthful diet and began exercising more.

"A lot of what I've been able to accomplish in golf is a direct result of becoming physically stronger," Tiger said. "I had to make my body complement my mind to make the most of my natural ability. In this game, you need every edge, and physical strength has definitely become one of mine."

Tiger played in only 11 tournaments in 1999, but he won eight of them, including the last four in a row. When he captured his first two tournaments in 2000, Tiger became the first player in nearly 50 years to win six consecutive events. Suddenly, his picture was on magazine covers everywhere, and crowds followed him both on and off the golf course. While the pressure increased, Tiger found a way to keep his concentration together. He developed a close friendship with pro basketball great Michael Jordan. Both men had a lot in common: each was driven to be the best in his sport, and each had trouble finding any privacy. They often spoke to each other by phone to discuss their problems.

Tiger's tremendous success on the fairway in 2000 drew comparisons to golf legend Bobby Jones, opposite bottom, who won the grand slam at age 28.

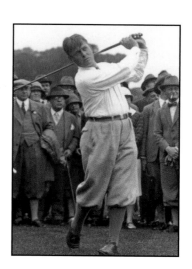

Tiger had his best year in 2000, when he captured three of the four major tournaments—the U.S. Open, British Open, and PGA Championship. Since he had already won the Masters in 1997, Tiger became only the fifth golfer in history to record a "career grand slam" by winning all four major events in his lifetime. After Tiger won his second Masters in April 2001, he became only the second golfer ever to reign as champion of all four majors at the same time. (The other was the legendary Bobby Jones, who won the grand slam in 1930.)

Tiger kept piling up victories and records throughout 2000, 2001, and 2002. His wins included a second U.S. Open and a third Masters, both in 2002. He also piled up prize money and endorsements from advertisers. Some experts predicted that Tiger would become the first athlete to earn more than a billion dollars in winnings and endorsements during his career.

But while Tiger and his family were proud of all of his sports and business accomplishments, they were even prouder of the changes he had brought to golf. He had helped to transform the mix of people who play and watch the sport. "I thought if I kept progressing in golf and came on the [PGA] tour and did really well, that I could help golf, bring more minorities into the game, and make it more diverse. I thought that would be my biggest impact. But the impact on kids is something else I really love," Tiger said.

Tiger Woods has changed the image of golf and created a special image for himself—as the game's greatest champion.

The son of African- and Asian-American parents, Tiger has inspired kids of all backgrounds to embrace their dreams, work hard, and make those dreams come true.

V O I C E S

ON HIS COMPETITIVE
NATURE:

"In my life, I've never gone to a tournament without thinking I could win. . . . That's just the mind-set I have. Each and every tournament, I go there to try and win, something I've always believed in, and I always will."

Tiger Woods

"He's an absolutely fearless competitor who wants to beat you, whether it's for $10,000 or $10 million, to prove, not to you but to himself, how good he is, which is this good: The world has not seen anything like this kid."

Rocco Mediate, PGA golfer

"Between my wife, Tiger, and me, Tiger has the hottest temper. He is the most competitive of the three of us. He'll compete in drinking a glass of water."

Earl Woods

"I know what I want to accomplish and I know how to get there. The ultimate goal is to be the best. Whether that's the best ever, who knows? I hope so."

Tiger Woods

ON HIS PLAYING STRATEGY:

"Sometimes, knowing where not to hit the golf ball is just as important as knowing where to hit it. This means playing away from trouble, especially off the tee."

Tiger Woods

"I always think out each shot carefully, usually from the green back, and pay particular attention to positioning for the best angle of attack to the flagstick. For instance, if I am faced with water on the left and deep rough on the right, I'll aim right to take double-bogey out of the equation. It sounds simple, but most average golfers just swing away without a game plan."

Tiger Woods

"I might not show it, but I get really pumped any time I can save a stroke. As Pop always says, 'Golf is like banking. Once you make a deposit, do your absolute best not to make a withdrawal.' That's why a par-saving 10-footer is as satisfying to me as a 40-foot snake for birdie."

Tiger Woods

Admired for his winning smile, phenomenal resume, and multiracial appeal, Tiger has endorsed products for such companies as Nike, Buick, and American Express.

ON HIS FEELINGS ABOUT GOLF:

"You know, if it wasn't fun I'd give it up. It's one of those things where if you're not having fun and enjoying what you're doing out here, there's really no sense in doing it. I thoroughly love playing. I love competing. And I love to try and find some way to get better."

Tiger Woods

"Golf humbles you every day, every shot, really. I know how hard the game is."

Tiger Woods

ON HIS RELATIONSHIP WITH HIS PARENTS:

"I never treated Tiger like a kid. I treated Tiger as an equal. We transcended the parent-child relationship and became best friends a long time ago."

Earl Woods

"You know, I think his [my father's] only dreams for me were to be honest and happy, and, if I were those two things, then his dreams were fulfilled. I am that. I'm truthful to people, and I couldn't be happier. I'm doing something I love to do every day."

Tiger Woods

The strategies and values behind Tiger's "Start Something" motivational program for kids are based on his father's book Start Something: You Can Make a Difference.

"I think people have a misunderstanding of my family. People think it was my dad who disciplined me, who was the one who was always so hard on me, insisting I do things by the letter. It was actually my mom. It was my mom who was always so by-the-book. She's the one who taught me how to be disciplined."

Tiger Woods

Whether teaming up with fellow golfers, such as Paul Azinger, above left, or competing against them, Tiger plays to win.

ON HIS ABILITY:

"He's Michael Jordan in long pants. He not only hits better than us, he thinks better than us."

Paul Azinger, PGA golfer

"There isn't a flaw in his golf or his makeup. He will win more majors than Arnold Palmer and I combined. Somebody is going to dust my records. It might as well be Tiger, because he's such a great kid."

Jack Nicklaus, golf legend

"We have to go back to the drawing board and make the holes bigger for us and a little smaller for him."

Ernie Els, PGA golfer

"Woods' arsenal includes the uncanny ability to outthink opponents and a cold-blooded streak, a la Jack Nicklaus, whereby the only place is first place."

Bob Verdi, sportswriter

● ON HIS LEGACY:

"Tiger . . . will succeed and expand across all racial barriers. . . . I admire him . . . for establishing a new plateau, a higher ground, if you will. . . . I really do believe he was put here for a bigger reason than just to play golf."

Michael Jordan,
former pro basketball star

"The smiles on the faces of kids grateful to get a few minutes of instruction [at clinics] warm my heart. I'm grateful to golf for giving me that feeling. In the big picture, what truly matters is the lives we touch."

Tiger Woods

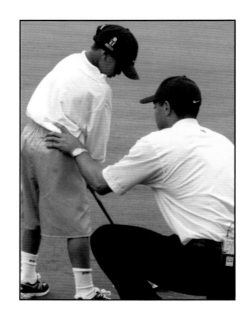

Generous with both his time and money, Tiger has given golf a fresh look and style, winning the respect of fellow golfers such as Jack Nicklaus, top, and Ernie Els, middle.

OVATIONS